P9-CND-491

Carolrhoda Books, Inc./Minneapolis

*For Joe Lucas*
*—L.L.*

*For Susan Nees, inspiring artist and faithful friend*
*—B.K.*



*This book is available in two editions:*
Library binding by Carolrhoda Books, Inc., a division of Lerner Publishing Group
Soft cover by First Avenue Editions, an imprint of Lerner Publishing Group
241 First Avenue North
Minneapolis, MN 55401 U.S.A.

Website address: www.lernerbooks.com

Library of Congress Cataloging-in-Publication Data

Lowery, Linda.
Day of the Dead / by Linda Lowery ; illustrations by Barbara Knutson.
p. cm. — (On my own holidays)
Summary: Introduces the holiday, Day of the Dead, or Dia de los Muertos, and describes how it is celebrated in Mexico and in the United States.
ISBN: 0–87614–914–X (lib. bdg. : alk. paper)
ISBN: 1–57505–581–3 (pbk. : alk. paper)
1. All Souls' Day—Mexico—Juvenile literature. [1. All Souls' Day. 2. Holidays.]
I. Knutson, Barbara, ill. II. Title. III. Series.
GT4995.A4 L69 2004
394.266—dc21 2002003011

Manufactured in the United States of America
1 2 3 4 5 6 – DP – 09 08 07 06 05 04

It is autumn.
Where are the bright summer flowers?
Where are the green leaves?
Where is the corn that grew tall
and turned ripe in the fields?

The flowers and leaves and corn
of summer are all gone.
They have died and gone back
to the earth.
All over North America,
people are celebrating.

In places like Mexico City, Los Angeles,
and New York, they are very busy.
They are getting ready for
El Dia de los Muertos,
the Day of the Dead.
They are celebrating death!

Does that sound strange to you?
It is not strange to the Mexican people,
the Cajun people, and others
who celebrate death.
They know that death brings new life.
The flower seeds will sprout new flowers.
The cornhusks will make the earth rich
for new corn.
When spring comes,
new life will sprout up everywhere.

People are the same way.
Like the leaves, the flowers, and the corn,
people also die.
But they leave behind gifts for the earth.
These gifts may be friends or family
whose lives they touched.
They may be children and grandchildren
and great-grandchildren.

Where would you be without the family members who came before you?

Think about it.

You would not be here!

Isn't that worth celebrating?

Day of the Dead is not a sad time.

It is a warm and loving time to remember people who have died.

It is a time to be thankful for life.

From the beginning of time, people have
celebrated the circle of life and death.
In Mexico, Aztec Indians celebrated
life and death hundreds of years ago.
They invited their dead relatives
to visit them each autumn.
They could not see these dead spirits.
But they believed they could feel them
all around.

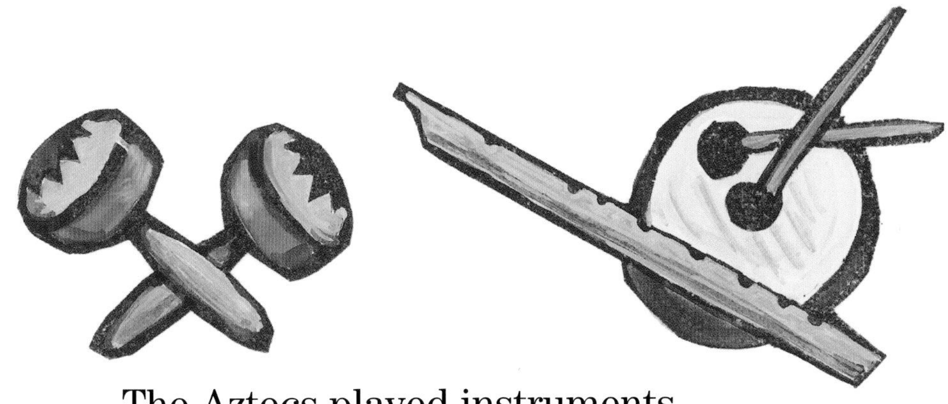

The Aztecs played instruments
made of turtle shells and dried gourds.
They carved twigs into flutes.
They lit candles and left food
for the spirits.
They thought the flames and the music
would guide the dead home.
They believed the spirits would happily
feast on their food.

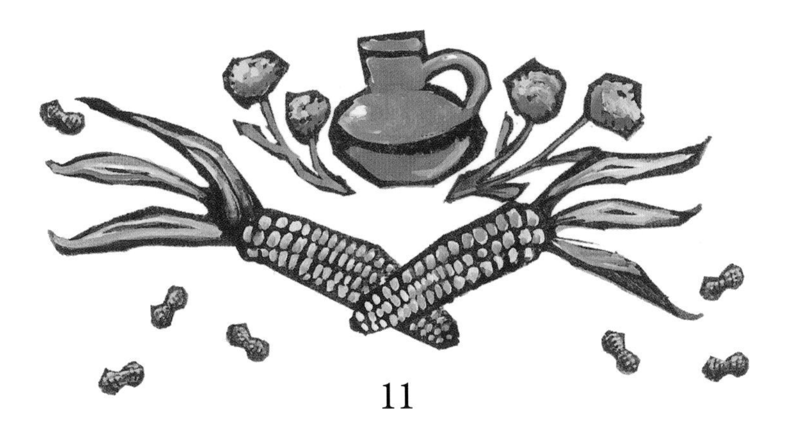

In 1521, Spanish explorers took control
of Mexico.
They had their own Christian celebrations.
November 1 was All Saints Day.
On that day, Spanish people went to
church to honor saints who had died.
November 2 was All Souls Day.
On that day, Spanish people prayed
for friends and family who had died.
The Spanish explorers wanted the Aztecs
to celebrate the same way.
They tried to stamp out Day of the Dead.
But the Aztecs held on to the beliefs
they had practiced for centuries.

In time, the Aztec and Spanish
celebrations combined.
Day of the Dead
became a Mexican holiday.
It is a three-day holiday in many places
in Mexico.
Most people celebrate from October 31
until November 2.
In the United States, Day of the Dead is
usually only one day, November 2.
But every city and town is different.

*October 31*

In a small town in Mexico,
mothers and grandmothers are busy.
They are preparing
a Day of the Dead feast.
Close your eyes and smell.
Sauce is simmering on the stove.

It smells like chilies and nuts, tomatoes
and . . . chocolate!
It is called mole.

The mole will flavor the tamales de mole.
Tamales are spicy meat wrapped up snug
in cornhusks.

What else do you smell?
Sweet bread is baking.
It smells like yeast and sugar
and oranges.
It is called pan de muertos,
bread of the dead.

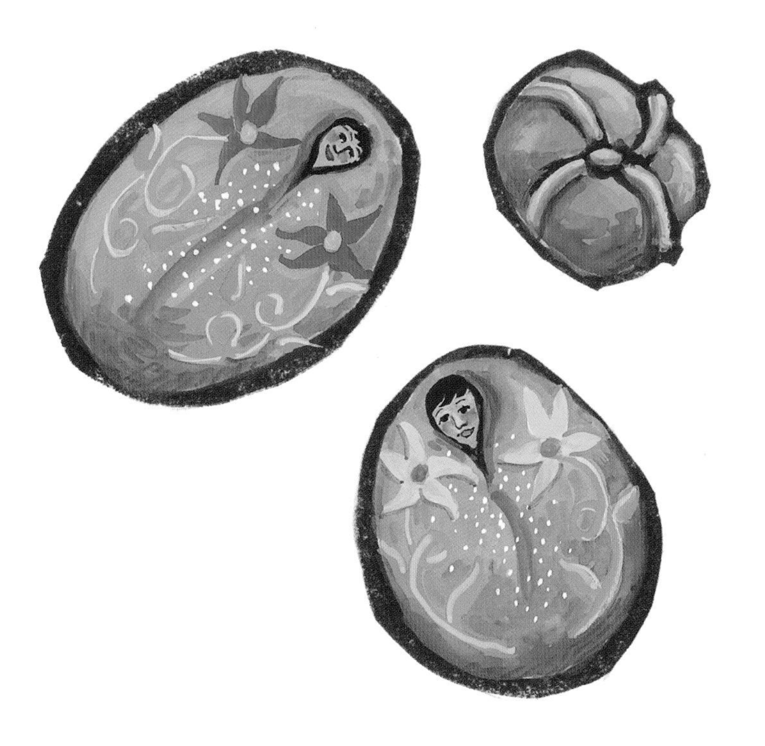

You can bake it in the shape of little
bodies wrapped in blankets.
You can shape it round like a skull
or long and skinny like a bone.
Sometimes there is a tiny sugar skull
or a candy skeleton hidden inside.

Look around you.
What do you see?
Farmers are driving into town.
Their trucks are heaped
with autumn flowers to sell.
The farmers have grown the flowers
especially for Day of the Dead.

The bouquets are as big as children.
Most of the flowers
are bright orange marigolds.
The Aztecs thought that orange was
the sacred color of the land of the dead.
They called marigolds
the flowers of the dead.

What else do you see?
At the market and in the shops,
people are selling candy and toys.
Even these treats honor the dead.
There are sugar coffins
with skeletons lying inside.
There are chocolate skulls.
There are toy skeletons
made of wood or paper.
These skeletons are called calacas.

They are not spooky like Halloween toys.
Calacas are silly and fun.
They are busy doing everyday things.
Some skeletons play guitars.
Some skeletons drive shiny red trucks.
There are bony brides and grooms
getting married.

On October 31,
everyone is preparing for night.
When dark falls,
what do you hear?
Boom! Fireworks crack in the sky.
Clang! Church bells ring.
Some towns mix Halloween fun
with Day of the Dead traditions.
Children dress up in costumes.

They are ghosts and angels and devils.
The children haunt the neighborhood,
collecting candy and fruit.
In Mexico they do not say
“Trick or Treat!”
They holler, “Calaveras!”
Calaveras means “skulls” in Spanish.
It reminds children that they are
celebrating people who have died.

In some places, older children carry
a coffin down the street.
Inside is a real teenage boy or girl.
The teenager is dressed up like
someone who has died.

People toss money, fruit, and candy
into the coffin.
"Gracias!" shouts the dead body,
with a happy smile.

*November 1*

Every autumn, monarch butterflies
fly south to Mexico.
They leave behind the cold of Canada
and the United States.
The first monarchs begin to appear
just in time for Day of the Dead.
Some people say that the monarchs are
the spirits of children who have died.
Many Mexicans believe that children
become little angels when they die.

They call the angels angelitos.
To welcome the angelitos,
families make an altar on a table at home.
The altar is a collection of treasures to
remind families of those who have died.
The altar for the angelitos is usually
prepared on November 1.
It is full of things the angelitos will like.

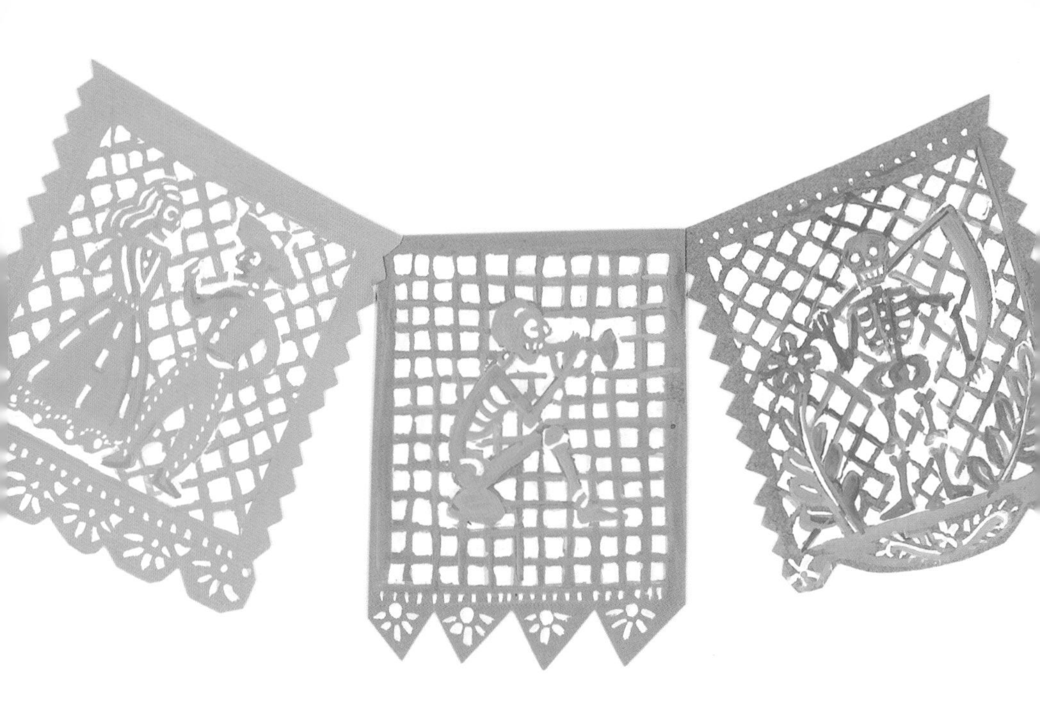

First, families lay down bright-colored
tissue paper.
Then they hang paper banners
called papel picado.
Each papel picado has been cut with
beautiful designs of skulls and skeletons.
They add toys and photographs taken of
the angelitos when they lived on earth.
Now come the angelitos' favorite foods.

There is pizza with lots of cheese.
There are sugar skulls and pink sugar watermelon slices.
There is a tiny cup of cocoa.
Won't the angelitos be happy to see all the things they love best?
Some people light firecrackers outside.
They hope the sparkles will help the angelitos find their way in the dark.

*November 2*

In the United States, today is the day
most people celebrate Day of the Dead.
There are lots of parades,
just as there are in Mexico.
Some towns have slow funeral parades,
with clarinets and drums.

Other parades are noisy and fun,
with costumes, masks, and music.
People watch the fun and sip atole,
a corn drink.

In small towns and big cities,
there are knocks on doors.
Who is there?
It is friends and family.
They come in,
bringing laughter, hugs, and gifts.
The gifts are photographs of loved ones,
favorite foods, candles, and flowers.
They are set on the home altar.
Friends and family sit around the altar.
They share stories about those
who have died.

In Mexico, families also build altars at the
cemeteries where loved ones are buried.
Fathers bring rakes, shovels, and brooms.
They weed and clean las tumbas,
the graves.
Now they will be tidy for the spirits
coming back for their yearly visit.
Everyone carries huge bouquets of
flowers to honor and welcome the dead.

They put them in tin cans and place them
on the graves.
Soon the whole graveyard is a garden
of red and yellow, white and purple.
Orange flowers are mixed
with green leaves.
The color of death mixes
with the color of life.

When evening comes,
it's time for picnics in the cemetery.
Baskets are opened.
Out comes the food.
There are tamales de mole,
pan de muertos, roasted peppers,
tortillas, atole, and candy.
Many families eat the food on tablecloths
spread out by the graves.
They leave extra food
for the visiting spirits.
Other families simply set their food out
on the altars.
They hope it will be enjoyed
by loved ones who visit in the night.

When night falls, the families light
candles all around the graves.
Now the cemetery is lit up
like a birthday cake in the dark.

Will those in the other world see
the flickering flames?
Music fills the air.
Some families play radios quietly.
Others strum guitars and sing.

In some places, boys dance
the Dance of the Little Old Men.
They hobble around with canes.
They hold their backs in pain.
They wear masks that look like
funny old men.

As the dance continues,
the dancers become young.
They stomp and strut merrily.
They are full of joy and life.
Will loved ones hear the music
and come to dance?

Many people stay all night
in the graveyard.
Children play games by candlelight.
Families share stories about loved ones.
Some stories are adventurous
or inspiring.

Some are funny and silly.
Remember how Grandma used to laugh so hard, she cried?
Remember how Great-Grandpa risked his life for freedom during the war?

These stories will be told by children
to their own children someday.
That way, the loved ones
are never forgotten.
Year after year, they will always
be remembered.

Year after year,
they will remind the children
that life is a great gift.
On Day of the Dead,
and every day,
how wonderful it is to be alive!

# Spanish Words

**angelitos** (ahn-hay-LEE-tohs): little angels

**atole** (ah-TOH-lay): Mexican drink made of corn

**calacas** (kah-LAH-kahs): handmade skeleton figures

**calaveras** (kah-lah-VAY-rahs): skulls

**El Dia de los Muertos** (EHL DEE-ah DAY LOHS MWEHR-tohs): Day of the Dead

**gracias** (GRAH-see-yahs): thank you

**las tumbas** (LAHS TOOM-bahs): graves

**pan de muertos** (PAHN DAY MWEHR-tohs): bread of the dead

**papel picado** (pah-PEHL pee-KAH-doh): cut paper banners

**tamales de mole** (tah-MAH-lays DAY MOHL-lay): spicy meat in cornhusks, served with sauce

**tortillas** (tohr-TEE-yahs): a round, flat bread made of cornmeal or flour